The Fear of God

by

George MacDonald

Rise of Douai

ISBN-13: 978-1519194480

ISBN-10: 151919448X

Introduction

George MacDonald (10 December 1824 – 18 September 1905) was a Scottish author, poet, and Christian minister. He was a pioneering figure in the field of fantasy literature and the mentor of fellow writer Lewis Carroll. His writings have been cited as a major literary influence by many notable authors including W. H. Auden, C. S. Lewis, J. R. R. Tolkien, Walter de la Mare, E. Nesbit and Madeleine L'Engle. C. S. Lewis wrote that he regarded MacDonald as his "master": "Picking up a copy of Phantastes one day at a train-station bookstall, I began to read. A few hours later," said Lewis, "I knew that I had crossed a great frontier." G. K. Chesterton cited The Princess and the Goblin as a book that had "made a difference to my whole existence".

Elizabeth Yates wrote of Sir Gibbie, "It moved me the way books did when, as a child, the great gates of literature began to open and first encounters with noble thoughts and utterances were unspeakably thrilling."

Even Mark Twain, who initially disliked MacDonald, became friends with him, and there is some evidence that Twain was influenced by MacDonald. Christian author Oswald Chambers (1874–1917) wrote in Christian Disciplines, vol. 1, (pub. 1934) that "it is a striking indication of the trend and shallowness of the modern reading public that George MacDonald's books have been so neglected".

In addition to his fairy tales, MacDonald wrote several works on Christian apologetics including several that defended his view of Christian Universalism.

George MacDonald's best-known works are Phantastes, The Princess and the Goblin, At the Back of the North Wind, and Lilith, all fantasy novels, and fairy tales such as "The Light Princess", "The Golden Key", and "The Wise Woman". "I write, not for children," he wrote, "but for the child-like, whether they be of five, or fifty, or seventy-five." MacDonald also published some volumes of sermons, the pulpit not having proved an unreservedly successful venue.

MacDonald also served as a mentor to Lewis Carroll (the pen-name of Rev. Charles Lutwidge Dodgson); it was MacDonald's advice, and the enthusiastic reception of Alice by MacDonald's many sons and daughters, that convinced Carroll to submit Alice for publication. Carroll, one of the finest Victorian photographers, also created photographic portraits of several of the MacDonald children.

MacDonald was also friends with John Ruskin and served as a go-between in Ruskin's long courtship with Rose La Touche.

MacDonald was acquainted with most of the literary luminaries of the day; a surviving group photograph shows him with Tennyson, Dickens, Wilkie Collins, Trollope, Ruskin, Lewes, and Thackeray. While in America he was a friend of Longfellow and Walt Whitman.

The Fear of God

And when I saw him, I fell at his feet as one dead. And he laid his right hand upon me, saying, Fear not; I am the first and the last and the Living one.'--Rev. i. 17, 18.

It is not alone the first beginnings of religion that are full of fear. So long as love is imperfect, there is room for torment. That lore only which fills the heart--and nothing but love can fill any heart--is able to cast out fear, leaving no room for its presence. What we find in the beginnings of religion, will hold in varying degree, until the religion, that is the love, be perfected.

The thing that is unknown, yet known to be, will always be more or less formidable. When it is known as immeasurably greater than we, and as having claims and making demands upon us, the more vaguely these are apprehended, the more room is there for anxiety; and when the conscience is not clear, this anxiety may well mount to terror. According to the nature of the mind which occupies itself with the idea of the Supreme, whether regarded as maker or ruler, will be the kind and degree of the terror. To this terror need belong no exalted ideas of God; those fear him most who most imagine him like their own evil selves, only beyond them in power, easily able to work his arbitrary will with them. That they hold him but a little higher than themselves, tends nowise to unity with him: who so far apart as those on the same level of hate and distrust? Power without love, dependence where is no righteousness, wake a worship without devotion, a loathliness of servile flattery. Neither, where the notion of God is better, but the conscience is troubled, will his goodness do much to exclude apprehension. The same consciousness of evil and of offence which gave rise to the bloody sacrifice, is still at work in the minds of most who call themselves Christians. Naturally the first emotion of man towards the being he calls God, but of whom he knows so little, is fear.

Where it is possible that fear should exist, it is well it should exist, cause continual uneasiness, and be cast out by nothing less than love. In him who does not know God, and must be anything but satisfied with himself, fear towards God is as reasonable as it is natural, and serves powerfully towards the development of his true humanity. Neither the savage, nor the self-sufficient sage, is rightly human. It matters nothing whether we regard the one or the other as degenerate or as undeveloped--neither I say is human; the humanity is there, but has to be born in each, and for this birth everything natural must do its part; fear is natural, and has a part to perform nothing but itself could perform in the birth of the true humanity. Until love, which is the truth towards God, is able to cast out fear, it is well that fear should hold; it is a bond, however poor, between that which is and that which creates--a bond that must be broken, but a bond that can be broken only by the tightening of an infinitely closer bond. Verily, God must be terrible to those that are far from him; for they fear he will do, yea, he is doing with them what they do not, cannot desire, and can ill endure. Such as many men are, such as all without God would become, they must prefer a devil, because of his supreme selfishness, to a God who will die for his creatures, and insists upon giving himself to them, insists upon their being unselfish and blessed like himself. That which is the power and worth of life they must be, or die; and the vague consciousness of this makes them afraid. They love their poor existence as it is; God loves it as it must be--and they fear him.

The false notions of men of low, undeveloped nature both with regard to what is good and what the Power requires of them, are such that they cannot but fear, and devotion is lost in the sacrifices of ingratiation: God takes them where they are, accepts whatever they honestly offer, and so helps them to outgrow themselves, preparing them to offer the true offering, and to know him whom they ignorantly worship. He will not abolish their fear except with the truth of his own being. Till they apprehend that, and in order that they may come to apprehend it, he receives their sacrifices of blood, the invention of their sore need, only influencing for the time the modes of them. He will destroy the lie that is not all a lie only by the truth which is all true. Although he loves them utterly, he does not tell them there is nothing in him to make them afraid. That would be to drive them from him for ever. While they are such as they are, there is much in him that cannot but affright them; they ought, they do well to fear him. It is, while they remain what they are, the only true relation between them. To remove that fear from their hearts, save by letting them know his love with its purifying fire, a love which for ages, it may be, they cannot know, would be to give them up utterly to the power of evil. Persuade men that fear is a vile thing, that it is an insult to God, that he will none of it--while yet they are in love with their own will, and slaves to every movement of passionate impulse, and what will the consequence be? That they will insult God as a discarded idol, a superstition, a falsehood, as a thing under whose evil influence they have too long groaned, a thing to be cast out and spit upon. After that how much will they learn of him? Nor would it be long ere the old fear would return--with this difference, perhaps, that instead of trembling before a live energy, they would tremble before powers which formerly they regarded as inanimate, and have now endowed with souls after the imagination of their fears. Then would spiritual chaos with all its monsters be come again. God being what he is, a God who loves righteousness; a God who, rather than do an unfair thing, would lay down his Godhead, and assert himself in ceasing to be; a God who, that his creature might not die of ignorance, died as much as a God could die, and that is divinely more than man can die, to give him himself; such a God, I say, may well look fearful from afar to the creature who recognizes in himself no imperative good; who fears only suffering, and has no aspiration--only wretched ambition! But in proportion as such a creature comes nearer, grows towards him in and for whose likeness he was begun; in proportion, that is, as the eternal right begins to disclose itself to him; in proportion as he becomes capable of the idea that his kind belongs to him as he could never belong to himself; approaches the capacity of seeing and understanding that his individuality can be perfected only in the love of his neighbour, and that his being can find its end only in oneness with the source from which it came; in proportion, I do not say as he sees these things, but as he nears the possibility of seeing them, will his terror at the God of his life abate; though far indeed from surmising the bliss that awaits him, he is drawing more nigh to the goal of his nature, the central secret joy of sonship to a God who loves righteousness and hates iniquity, does nothing he would not permit in his creature, demands nothing of his creature he would not do himself.

The fire of God, which is his essential being, his love, his creative power, is a fire unlike its earthly symbol in this, that it is only at a distance it burns--that the farther from him, it burns the worse, and that when we turn and begin to approach him, the burning begins to change to comfort, which comfort will grow to such bliss that the heart at length cries out with a gladness no other gladness can reach, 'Whom have I in heaven but thee? and there is none upon earth that I desire besides thee!' The glory of being, the essence of life and its joy, shining upon the corrupt and deathly, must needs, like the sun, consume the dead, and send corruption down to the dust; that which it burns in the soul is not of the soul, yea, is at utter variance with it; yet so close to the soul is the foul fungous growth sprung from and subsisting upon it, that the burning of it is felt through every spiritual nerve: when the evil parasites are consumed away, that is when the man yields his self and all that self's low world, and returns to his lord and God, then that which, before, he was aware of only as burning, he will feel as love, comfort, strength--an eternal, ever-growing life in him. For now he lives, and life cannot hurt life; it can only hurt death, which needs and ought to be destroyed. God is life essential, eternal, and death cannot live in his sight; for death is corruption, and has no existence in itself, living only in the decay of the things of life. If then any child of the father finds that he is afraid before him, that the thought of God is a discomfort to him, or even a terror, let him make haste--let him not linger to put on any garment, but rush at once in his nakedness, a true child, for shelter from his own evil and God's terror, into the salvation of the Father's arms, the home whence he was sent that he might learn that it was home. What father being evil would it not win to see the child with whom he was vexed running to his embrace? how much more will not the Father of our spirits, who seeks nothing but his children themselves, receive him with open arms!

Self, accepted as the law of self, is the one demon-enemy of life; God is the only Saviour from it, and from all that is not God, for God is life, and all that is not God is death. Life is the destruction of death, of all that kills, of all that is of death's kind.

When John saw the glory of the Son of Man, he fell at his feet as one dead. In what way John saw him, whether in what we vaguely call a vision, or in as human a way as when he leaned back on his bosom and looked up in his face, I do not now care to ask: it would take all glorious shapes of humanity to reveal Jesus, and he knew the right way to show himself to John. It seems to me that such words as were spoken can have come from the mouth of no mere vision, can have been allowed to enter no merely tranced ear, that the mouth of the very Lord himself spoke them, and that none but the living present Jesus could have spoken or may be supposed to speak them; while plainly John received and felt them as a message he had to give again. There are also, strangely as the whole may affect us, various points in his description of the Lord's appearance which commend themselves even to our ignorance by their grandeur and fitness. Why then was John overcome with terror? We recall the fact that something akin to terror overwhelmed the minds of the three disciples who saw his glory on the mount; but since then John had leaned on the bosom of his Lord, had followed him to the judgment seat and had not denied his name, had borne witness to his resurrection and suffered for his sake--and was now 'in the isle that is called Patmos, for the word of God and the testimony of Jesus:' why, I say, was he, why should he be afraid? No glory even of God should breed terror; when a child of God is afraid, it is a sign that the word Father is not yet freely fashioned by the child's spiritual mouth. The glory can breed terror only in him who is capable of being terrified by it; while he is such it is well the terror should be bred and maintained, until the man seek refuge from it in the only place where it is not--in the bosom of the glory.

There is one point not distinguishable in the Greek:

whether is meant, 'one like unto the Son of Man,' or, 'one like unto a son of Man:' the authorized version has the former, the revised prefers the latter. I incline to the former, and think that John saw him like the man he had known so well, and that it was the too much glory, dimming his vision, that made him unsure, not any perceived unlikeness mingling with the likeness. Nothing blinds so much as light, and their very glory might well render him unable to distinguish plainly the familiar features of The Son of Man.

But the appearance of The Son of Man was not intended to breed terror in the son of man to whom he came. Why then was John afraid? why did the servant of the Lord fall at his feet as one dead? Joy to us that he did, for the words that follow--surely no phantasmic outcome of uncertain vision or blinding terror! They bear best sign of their source: however given to his ears, they must be from the heart of our great Brother, the one Man, Christ Jesus, divinely human!

It was still and only the imperfection of the disciple, unfinished in faith, so unfinished in everything a man needs, that was the cause of his terror. This is surely implied in the words the Lord said to him when he fell! The thing that made John afraid, he speaks of as the thing that ought to have taken from him all fear. For the glory that he saw, the head and hair pouring from it such a radiance of light that they were white as white wool--snow-white, as his garments on mount Hermon; in the midst of the radiance his eyes like a flame of fire, and his countenance as the sun shineth in his strength; the darker glow of the feet, yet as of fine brass burning in a furnace--as if they, in memory of the twilight of his humiliation, touching the earth took a humbler glory than his head high in the empyrean of undisturbed perfection; the girdle under his breast, golden between the snow and the brass;--what were they all but the effulgence of his glory who was himself the effulgence of the Father's, the poor expression of the unutterable verity which was itself the reason why John ought not to be afraid?--'He laid his right hand upon me, saying unto me, Fear not; I am the first and the last, and the living one.'

Endless must be our terror, until we come heart to heart with the fire- core of the universe, the first and the last and the living one!

But oh, the joy to be told, by Power himself, the first and the last, the living one--told what we can indeed then see must be true, but which we are so slow to believe--that the cure for trembling is the presence of Power; that fear cannot stand before Strength; that the visible God is the destruction of death; that the one and only safety in the universe, is the perfect nearness of the Living One! God is being; death is nowhere! What a thing to be taught by the very mouth of him who knows! He told his servant Paul that strength is made perfect in weakness; here he instructs his servant John that the thing to be afraid of is weakness, not strength. All appearances of strength, such as might rightly move terror, are but false appearances; the true Strong is the One, even as the true Good is the One. The Living One has the power of life; the Evil One but the power of death--whose very nature is a self-necessity for being destroyed.

But the glory of the mildest show of the Living One is such, that even the dearest of his apostles, the best of the children of men, is cowed at the sight. He has not yet learned that glory itself is a part of his inheritance, yea is of the natural condition of his being; that there is nothing in the man made in the image of God alien from the most glorious of heavenly shows: he has not learned this yet, and falls as dead before it-- when lo, the voice of him that was and is and is for evermore, telling him not to be afraid--for the very reason, the one only reason, that he is the first and the last, the living one! For what shall be the joy, the peace, the completion of him that lives, but closest contact with his Life?--a contact close as ere he issued from that Life, only in infinitely higher kind, inasmuch as it is now willed on both sides. He who has had a beginning, needs the indwelling power of that beginning to make his being complete--not merely complete to his consciousness, but complete in itself-- justified, rounded, ended where it began--with an 'endless ending.' Then is it complete even as God's is complete, for it is one with the self-existent, blossoming in the air of that world wherein it is rooted, wherein it lives and grows. Far indeed from trembling because he on whose bosom he had leaned when the light of his love was all but shut in now stands with the glory of that love streaming forth, John

Boanerges ought to have felt the more joyful and safe as the strength of the living one was more manifested. It was never because Jesus was clothed in the weakness of the flesh that he was fit to be trusted, but because he was strong with a strength able to take the weakness of the flesh for the garment wherein it could best work its work: that strength was now shining out with its own light, so lately pent within the revealing veil. Had John been as close in spirit to the Son of Man as he had been in bodily presence, he would have indeed fallen at his feet, but not as one dead--as one too full of joy to stand before the life that was feeding his; he would have fallen, but not to lie there senseless with awe the most holy; he would have fallen to embrace and kiss the feet of him who had now a second time, as with a resurrection from above, arisen before him, in yet heavenlier plenitude of glory.

It is the man of evil, the man of self-seeking design, not he who would fain do right, not he who, even in his worst time, would at once submit to the word of the Master, who is reasonably afraid of power. When God is no longer the ruler of the world, and there is a stronger than he; when there is might inherent in evil, and making-energy in that whose nature is destruction; then will be the time to stand in dread of power. But even then the bad man would have no security against the chance of crossing some scheme of the lawless moment, where disintegration is the sole unity of plan, and being ground up and destroyed for some no-idea of the Power of darkness. And then would be the time for the good--no, not to tremble, but to resolve with the Lord of light to endure all, to let every billow of evil dash and break upon him, nor do the smallest ill, tell the whitest lie for God--knowing that any territory so gained could belong to no kingdom of heaven, could be but a province of the kingdom of darkness. If there were two powers, the one of evil, the other of good, as men have not unnaturally in ignorance imagined, his sense of duty would reveal the being born of the good power, while he born of the evil could have no choice but be evil. But Good only can create; and if Evil were ever so much the stronger, the duty of men would remain the same--to hold by the Living One, and defy Power to its worst--like Prometheus on his rock, defying Jove, and for ever dying--thus for ever foiling the Evil. For Evil can destroy only itself and its own; it could destroy no enemy--could at worst but cause a succession of deaths, from each of which the defiant soul would rise to loftier defiance, to more victorious endurance-- until at length it laughed Evil in the face, and the demon-god shrunk withered before it. In those then who believe that good is the one power, and that evil exists only because for a time it subserves, cannot help subserving the good, what place can there be for fear? The strong and the good are one; and if our hope coincides with that of God, if it is rooted in his will, what should we do but rejoice in the effulgent glory of the First and the Last?

The First and the Last is the inclosing defence of the castle of our being; the Master is before and behind; he began, he will see that it be endless. He garrisons the place; he is the living, the live-making one.

The reason then for not fearing before God is, that he is all-glorious, all-perfect. Our being needs the all-glorious, all-perfect God. The children can do with nothing less than the Father; they need the infinite one. Beyond all wherein the poor intellect can descry order; beyond all that the rich imagination can devise; beyond all that hungriest heart could long, fullest heart thank for--beyond all these, as the heavens are higher than the earth, rise the thought, the creation, the love of the God who is in Christ, his God and our God, his Father and our Father.

Ages before the birth of Jesus, while, or at least where yet even Moses and his law were unknown, the suffering heart of humanity saw and was persuaded that nowhere else lay its peace than with the first, the last, the living one:--

O that thou woudest hide me in the grave,... and remember me!... Thou shalt call, and I will answer thee: thou wilt have a desire to the work of thine hands.

THE END

RISE OF DOUAI

RISE OF DOUAI

TWITTER : @RISEOFDOUAI

© 2013, PUBLISHED BY RISE OF DOUAI PUBLISHING, OTHER PUBLICATIONS:

- AN IDIOT'S GUIDE TO: BEE HUNTING BY JOHN LOCKARD, EDITED BY ARSALAN AHMED (2012)(PAPERBACK) ISBN-10: 1478383550

- THE RISE OF DOUAI BY ARSALAN AHMED (2012)(PAPERBACK) ISBN-10: 1479267783

- THE RICHEST MAN IN BABYLON BY GEORGE S. CLASON (2012) (PAPERBACK) ISBN-10: 1479377341

- THINK AND GROW RICH BY NAPOLEON HILL (2012) (PAPERBACK) ISBN-10: 1480061638

- AS A MAN THINKETH BY MR JAMES ALLEN (2012) (PAPERBACK) ISBN-10: 1480088161
- HOW TO ANALYZE PEOPLE ON

SIGHT BY ELSIE BENEDICT (PAPERBACK) ISBN-10: 1480081272

- THE ART OF WAR BY MR SUN TZU (PAPERBACK) ISBN-10: 1480082007
- MACBETH BY MR WILLIAM SHAKESPEARE (PAPERBACK) ISBN-10: 1480060682
- A CHRISTMAS CAROL BY MR CHARLES DICKENS ISBN-10: 1481194755
- CREATING CAPITAL: MONEY-MAKING AS AN AIM IN BUSINESS BY MR FREDRICK L LIPMAN ISBN-10: 1481158996
- GETTING GOLD: A PRACTICAL TREATISE FOR PROSPECTORS, MINERS, AND STUDENTS BY MR JOSEPH COLIN FRANCIS JOHNSON ISBN-10: 1481090984
- THE INTERPRETATION OF DREAMS BY MR SIGMUND FREUD ISBN-10: 1481134558
- THE COMMUNIST MANIFESTO BY MR KARL MARX AND MR FRIDRICK ENGLES ISBN-10:

1480112445
- THE PRINCE BY MR NICCOLO MACHIAVELLI ISBN-10: 1480119601
- THE WAY TO WEALTH BY MR BENJAMIN FRANKLIN ISBN-10: 1480099651
- THE ART OF MONEY GETTING - OR GOLDEN RULES FOR MAKING MONEY (SUCCESS PRINCIPLES) BY MR PHINEAS TAYLOR BARNUM ISBN-10: 1480138622

Twitter : **@RiseofDouai**

Made in the USA
Las Vegas, NV
07 March 2022

45211943R00015